THE BIGGEST

ENGINEERING FAILURES

by Connie Colwell Miller

CAPSTONE PRESS
a capstone imprint

Blazers Books are published by Capstone Press,
1710 Roe Crest Drive, North Mankato, Minnesota 56003
www.mycapstone.com

Library of Congress Cataloging-in-Publication data
Library of Congress Cataloging-in-Publication data is available on the
ibrary of Congress website.
ISBN 978-1-5157-9990-0 (library binding)
ISBN 978-1-5157-9994-8 (paperback)
ISBN 978-1-5157-9999-3 (eBook PDF)

Editorial Credits
Mandy Robbins, editor; Bobbie Nuytten, designer; Morgan Walters,
media researcher; Tori Abraham, production specialist

Photo Credits
ASSOCIATED PRESS, 17; Getty Images: Bettmann, 19, 21, Boston
Globe, 13, East News, 25, Haynes Archive/Popperfoto, 15; Library of
Congress: Prints and Photographs Division, 7, 23, 27; Newscom: LARRY
DOWNING/REUTERS, 11, NASA/UPI, 9; Shutterstock: Crystal-K,
(people) design element throughout, Great Siberia Studio, (tsunami
wave) Cover, jctabb, (waterfall) Cover, Maciej Bledowski, (hover
dam) Cover, MasterBent_cameraman, 5, Monkey Business Images, 28,
photocell, (brass plate) design element throughout, Ruben Martinez
Barricarte, (waterfall) Cover, sergio34, (water) Cover, tonkid, 29

Printed and bound in the United States of America.
010753S18

Table of Contents

Design Disasters 4

Tacoma Narrows Bridge Collapse. . 6

The *Challenger* Explosion 8

I-35 Bridge Collapse 10

Boston Molasses Disaster 12

R101 Airship Disaster 14

Hyatt Regency Hotel
   Walkway Collapse 16

East Ohio Gas Explosion 18

The St. Francis Dam Disaster 20

The Johnstown Flood 22

Chernobyl 24

Banqiao Reservoir Dam
   Collapse 26

A Safer Future 28

   Glossary. 30

   Read More 31

   Internet Sites 31

   Index 32

Design Disasters

Engineers are people who design buildings and other structures. Sometimes engineers make mistakes. These errors can lead to disaster. Some of the worst mistakes have cost people their lives.

Tacoma Narrows Bridge Collapse

In 1940 a *suspension bridge* in Tacoma, Washington, *collapsed*. Its designers had not planned for high wind forces. Luckily, there was just one car on the bridge when it fell. The only death was a dog.

suspension bridge—a bridge hung from cables or chains strung from towers

collapse—to fall down suddenly

The collapse of the Tacoma Narrows Bridge was caught by a photographer.

Fact:
The bridge was nicknamed "Galloping Gertie" because it often swung in the wind.

The *Challenger* Explosion

In 1986 the space shuttle *Challenger* exploded 73 seconds after **liftoff**. All seven astronauts inside died. Bad O-rings caused the explosion. These parts seal in hot gas. Project managers had ignored warnings from engineers about them.

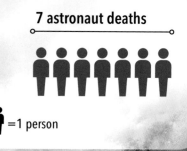

7 astronaut deaths

👤 =1 person

liftoff—the movement of a spacecraft as it rises off the ground

Challenger *took off the morning of January 28, 1986.*

Fact:

Challenger was carrying schoolteacher Christa McAuliffe. She would have been the first teacher in space.

I-35 Bridge Collapse

A design flaw caused a bridge to fall in Minneapolis, Minnesota, in 2007. *Construction* materials added extra weight to the bridge. It fell during rush hour. Thirteen people died, and 145 were injured.

13 deaths

♦ =1 person

construction—the process of building something

Fact:
The U.S. government has improved their bridge inspection process since the I-35 bridge disaster. Bridges are now usually inspected every two years.

Boston Molasses Disaster

In 1919 a 50-foot (15-meter) high storage tank in Boston burst. It was full of *molasses*. The tank had not been tested well before being filled. A wave of molasses flooded the city. It killed 21 people and injured 150 more.

21 deaths

👤👤👤👤👤👤👤👤👤👤👤👤👤👤👤👤👤👤👤👤👤

👤 =1 person

molasses—a thick, sweet syrup made when sugarcane is processed into sugar

Boston residents take in the aftermath of the molasses wave.

R101 Airship Disaster

The R101 *airship* had only been tested in good weather. In 1930 it took its first long journey. This time, strong winds tore into the ship. The gas bag ripped. The ship crashed and caught fire. In total 48 people died.

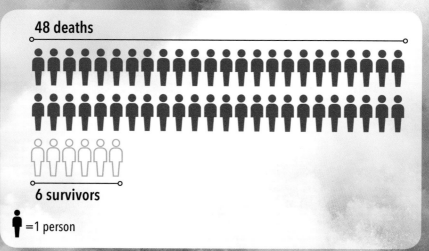

48 deaths

6 survivors

= 1 person

airship—a lighter-than-air aircraft with engines and a passenger compartment hanging underneath it

Men inspect the wreckage of the R101 airship crash.

Fact:
Only six people survived the R101 disaster.

Hyatt Regency Hotel Walkway Collapse

In 1981 a hotel in Kansas City, Missouri, held a large dance party in the main room. But the walkways above it had been built wrong. Two collapsed. The disaster killed 114 people. Another 200 were injured.

114 deaths

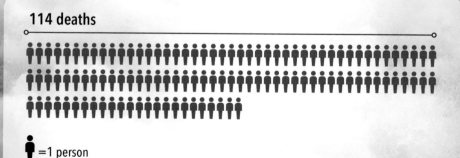

♟ =1 person

The entire main room of the Hyatt Regency Hotel was scattered with wreckage.

East Ohio Gas Explosion

In 1944 a natural gas storage tank began to leak in Cleveland, Ohio. The gas was stored at very cold temperatures. The cold made the metal in the tank *contract*. The leak caused two explosions. They killed 130 people.

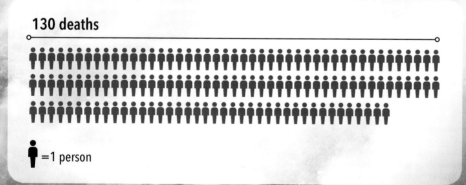

130 deaths

👤 =1 person

contract–to tighten and become shorter; metal contracts in cold temperatures

Fact:
One square mile (1.6 square kilometers) of Cleveland lay in ruins after the East Ohio Gas Company explosion.

The St. Francis Dam Disaster

In the 1920s William Mulholland led the construction of a dam in southern California. The dam was not strong enough when filled with water. It burst in 1928. A 10-story wall of water rushed out. It killed at least 450 people.

450 deaths

= 50 people

Fact:

The St. Francis Dam released
12.5 billion gallons (47.3 billion
liters) of water when it failed.

The Johnstown Flood

In 1889 a flood wiped out the city of Johnstown, Pennsylvania. A failure in the South Fork dam 14 miles (22.5 km) away was the cause. A giant wave of water and *debris* killed 2,209 people.

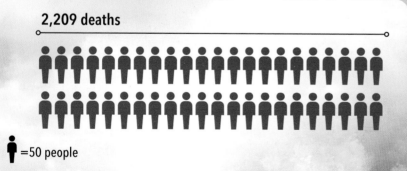

2,209 deaths

= 50 people

debris—the scattered pieces of something that has been broken or destroyed

A survivor stands on top of some of the wreckage of the Johnstown Flood.

Chernobyl

Chernobyl is the worst *nuclear* power plant accident in history. In 1986 a *reactor* exploded at the Nuclear Plant in Ukraine. The reactor had a design flaw. The explosion released dangerous nuclear energy. Around 4,000 people died.

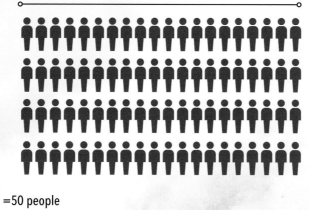

about 4,000 deaths

= 50 people

nuclear–describes energy converted by splitting two particles of matter

reactor–a large machine in which nuclear energy is produced by splitting atoms under controlled conditions

The explosion tore a giant hole in the Chernobyl Nuclear Plant.

Banqiao Reservoir Dam Collapse

In 1975 the River Ru in China flooded.
The Banqiao Reservoir Dam collapsed.
A wave up to 23 feet (7 m) high and
6 miles (10 km) wide destroyed the area.
About 171,000 people died.

about 171,000 deaths

ⓘ =1,000 people

Entire towns were wiped out when the River Ru flooded.

Fact:

At least one expert, Chen Xing, had warned the Chinese government that the dam wasn't safe.

A Safer Future

Engineering failures can be tragic. But people have learned from these mistakes. Engineers study these disasters. They want to make sure such tragedies never happen again.

Glossary

airship (AIR-ship)–a lighter-than-air aircraft with engines and a passenger compartment hanging underneath it

collapse (kuh-LAPS)–to fall down suddenly

construction (kuhn-STRUK-shuhn)–the process of building something

contract (kuhn-TRAKT)–to tighten and become shorter; metal contracts in cold temperatures

debris (duh-BREE)–the scattered pieces of something that has been broken or destroyed

liftoff (LIFT-off)–the movement of a spacecraft as it rises off the ground

molasses (muh-LASS-iz)–a thick, sweet syrup made when sugarcane is processed into sugar

nuclear (NOO-klee-ur)–describes energy converted by splitting two particles of matter

reactor (ree-AK-tur)–a large machine in which nuclear energy is produced by splitting atoms under controlled conditions

suspension bridge (suh-SPEN-shuhn BRIJ)–a bridge hung from cables or chains strung from towers

Read More

Nagelhout, Ryan. *The Hindenburg Disaster.* Doomed!
New York: Gareth Stevens Publishing, 2016.

Rice, Dona. *Engineering Marvels: the Eiffel Tower.*
Huntington Beach, Calif.: Teacher Created Materials, 2017.

Ventura, Marne. *Detecting Floods.* Detecting Disasters.
Mankato, Minn.: North Star Editions, 2017.

Internet Sites

Use FactHound to find Internet sites related to this book.

Visit *www.facthound.com*

Just type in 9781515799900 and go.

 Check out projects, games and lots more at
www.capstonekids.com

Index

Banqiao Reservoir Dam, 26
Boston Molasses disaster, 12

Challenger, 8, 9
Chen Xing, 27
Chernobyl, 24

East Ohio Gas Company
    explosion, 18, 19

Hyatt Regency Hotel, 16

I-35 bridge, 10, 11

Johnstown Flood, 22

McAuliffe, Christa, 9
Mulholland, William, 20

R101 airship, 14, 15

St. Francis Dam, 20, 21

Tacoma Narrows Bridge, 6, 7